ARTIST
TRANSCRIPTIONS
PIANO

A CHARLIE BROWN CHRISTMAS™

ISBN: 978-1-5400-2924-9

HAL•LEONARD®

Visit Hal Leonard Online at
www.halleonard.com

Contact Us:
Hal Leonard
7777 West Bluemound Road
Milwaukee, WI 53213
Email: info@halleonard.com

In Europe contact:
Hal Leonard Europe Limited
Distribution Centre, Newmarket Road
Bury St Edmunds, Suffolk, IP33 3YB
Email: info@halleonardeurope.com

In Australia contact:
Hal Leonard Australia Pty. Ltd.
4 Lentara Court
Cheltenham, Victoria, 3192 Australia
Email: info@halleonard.com.au

Christmas Is Coming

By Vince Guaraldi

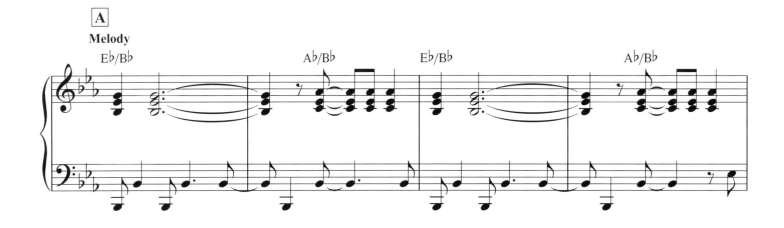

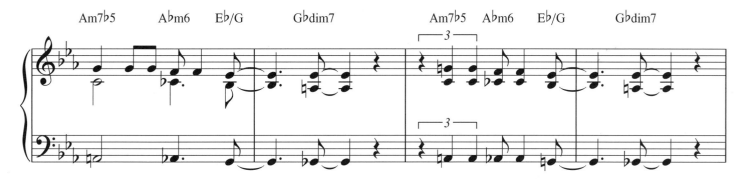

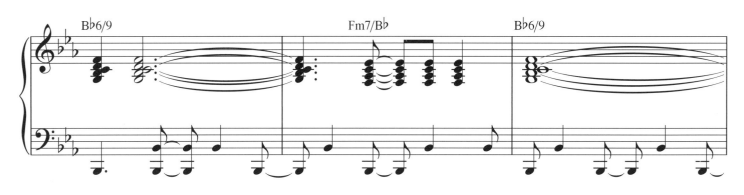

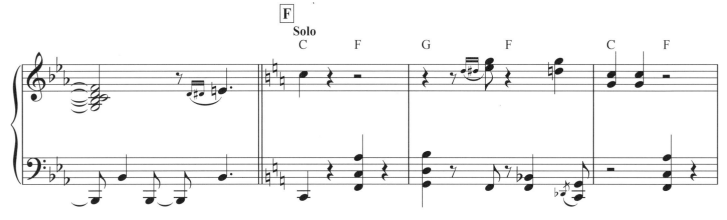

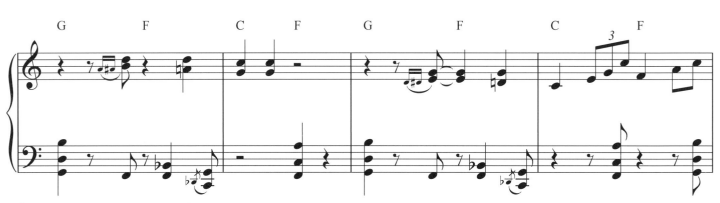

7

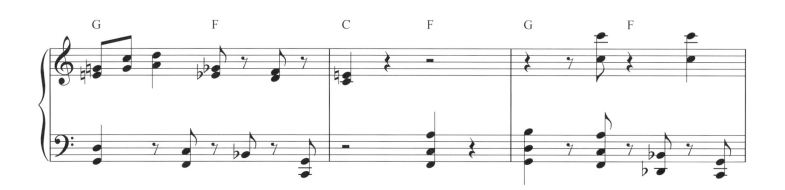

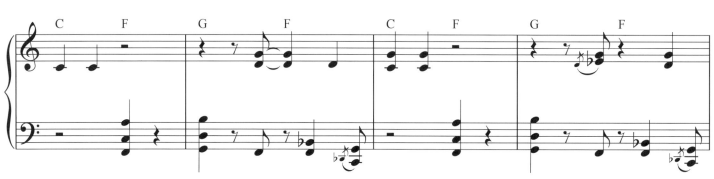

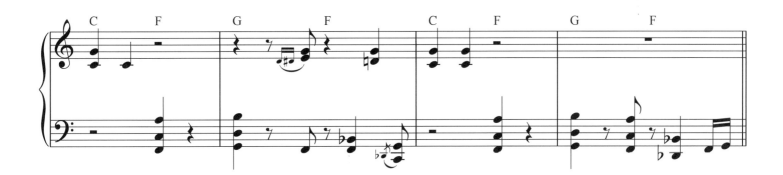

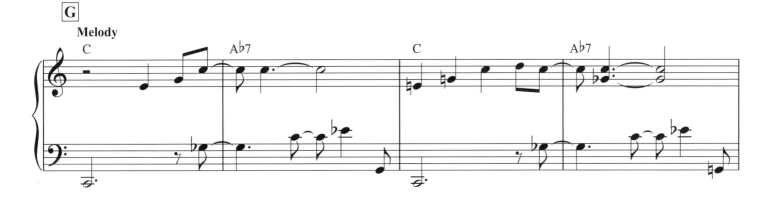

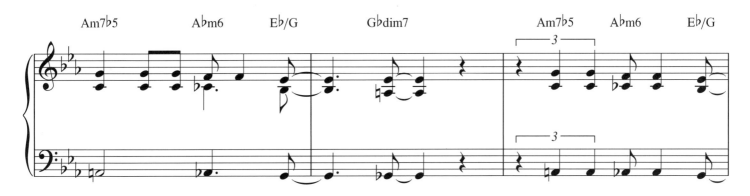

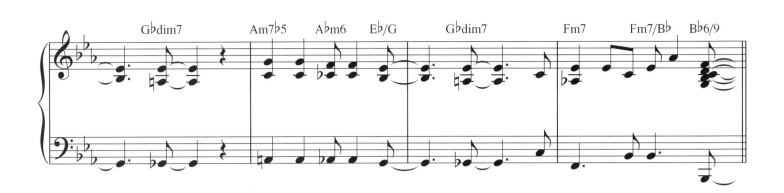

H
Outro

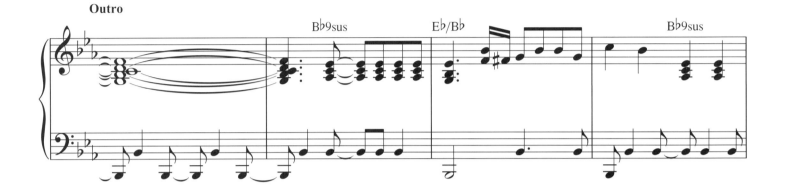

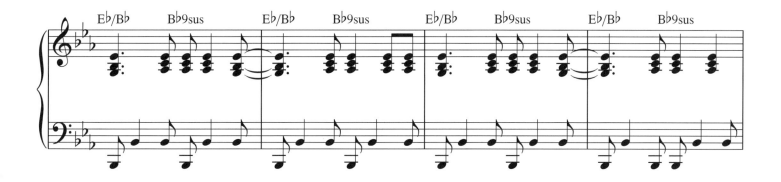

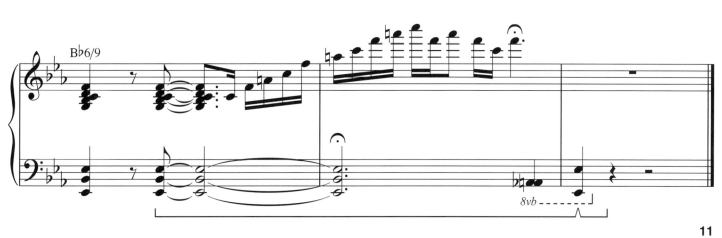

The Christmas Song

(Chestnuts Roasting on an Open Fire)

Music and Lyric by Mel Tormé and Robert Wells

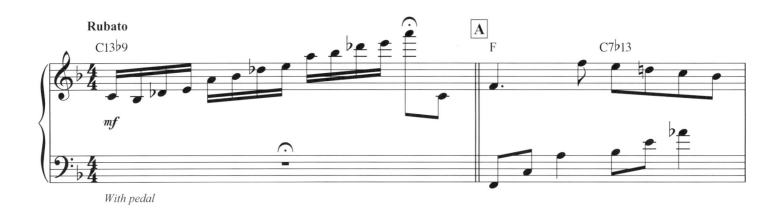

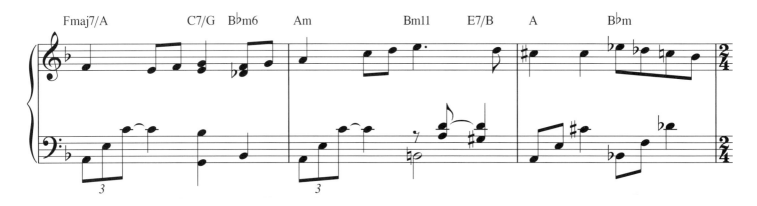

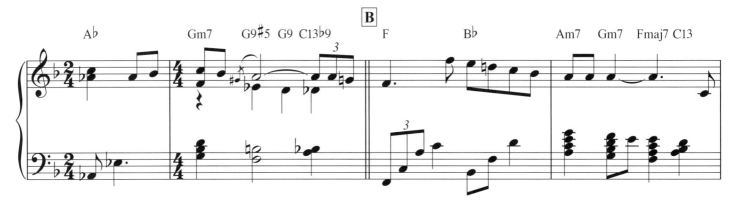

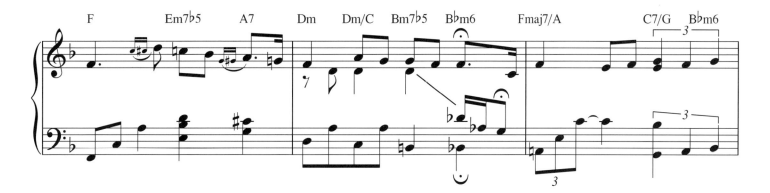

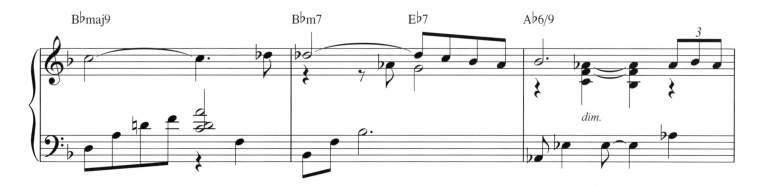

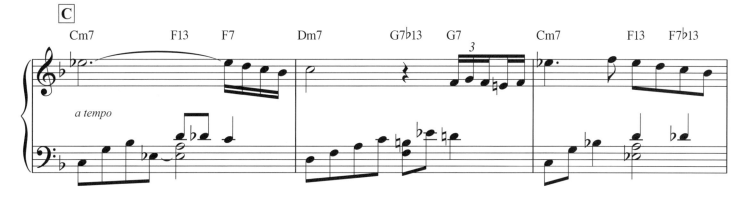

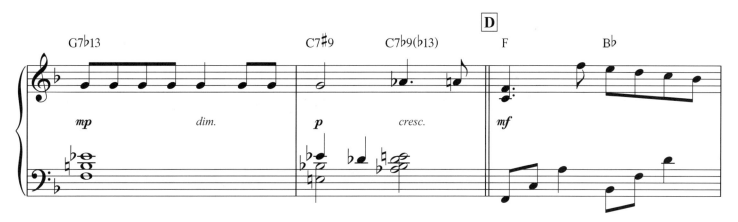

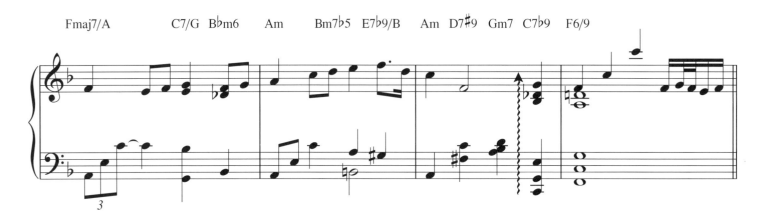

E Slowly

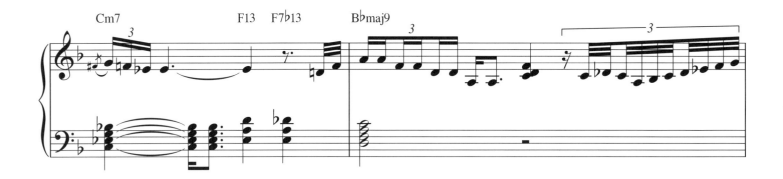

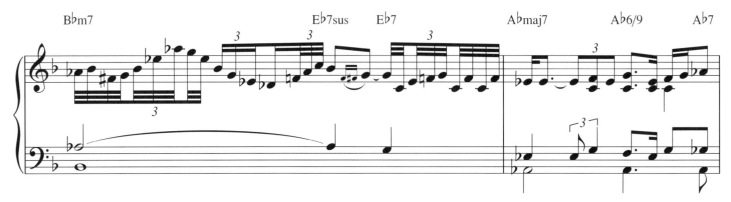

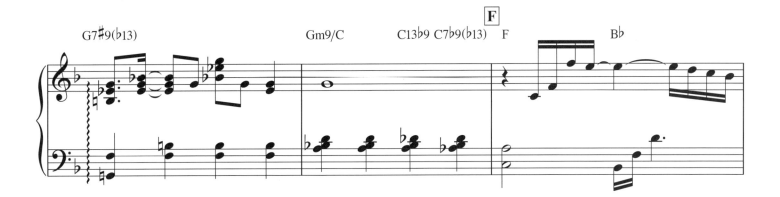

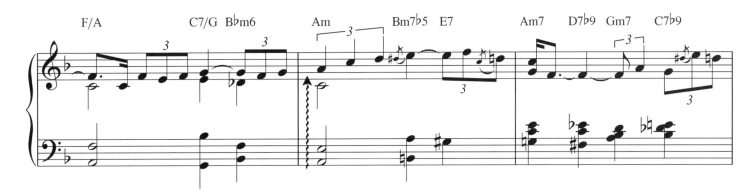

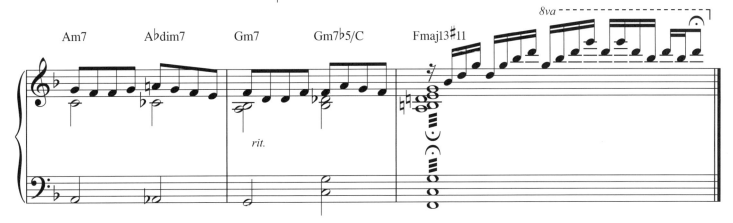

Christmas Time Is Here

Words by Lee Mendelson
Music by Vince Guaraldi

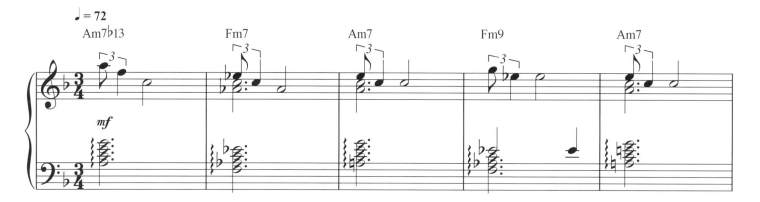

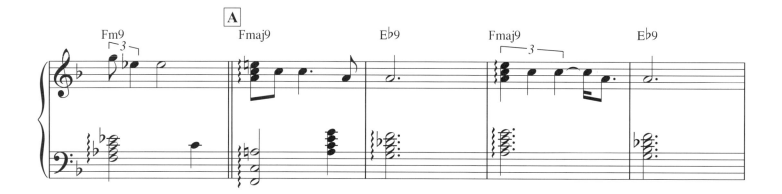

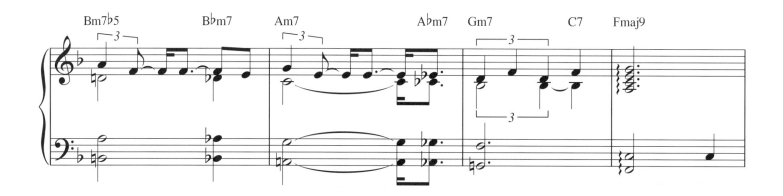

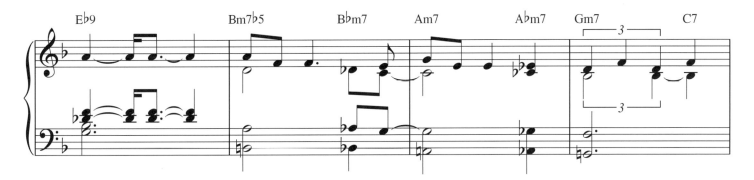

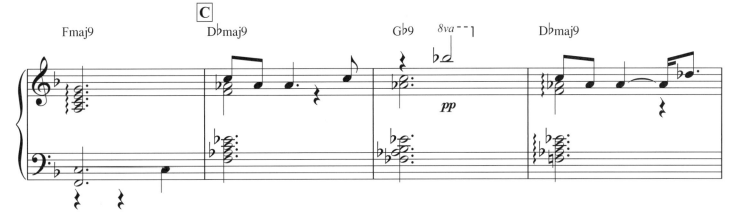

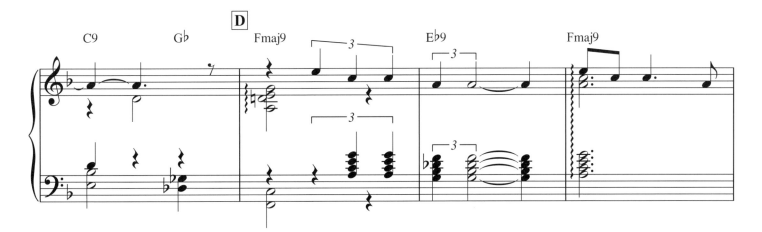

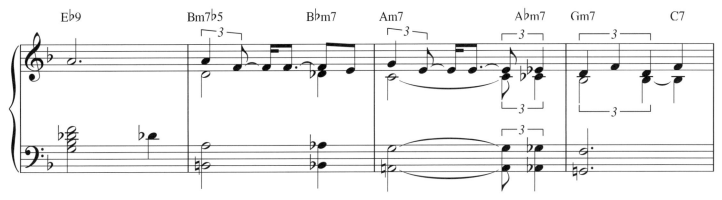

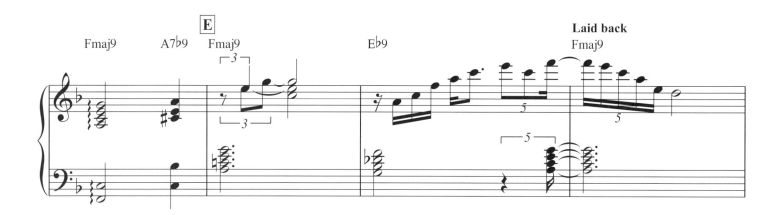

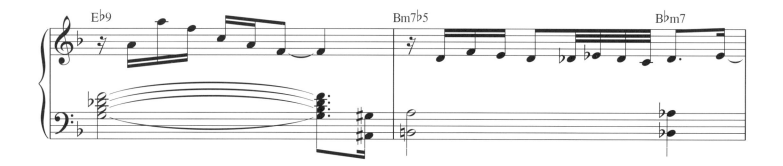

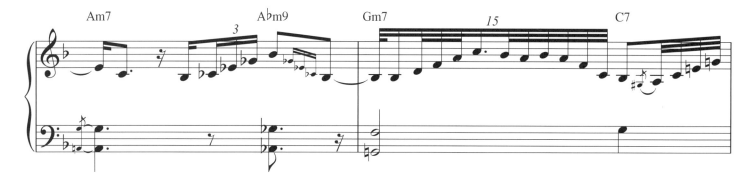

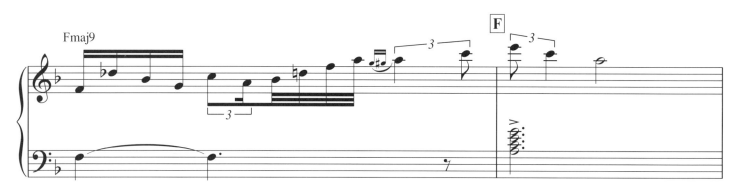

Laid Back

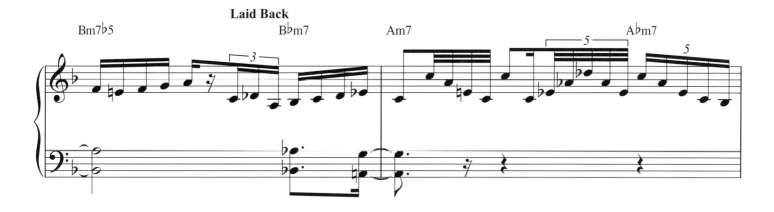

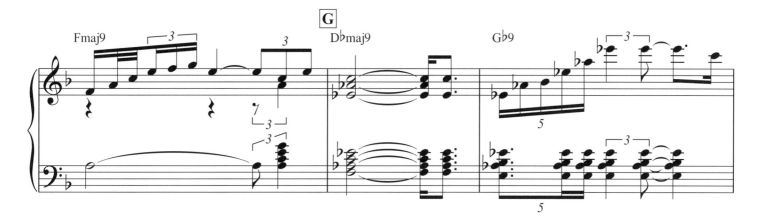

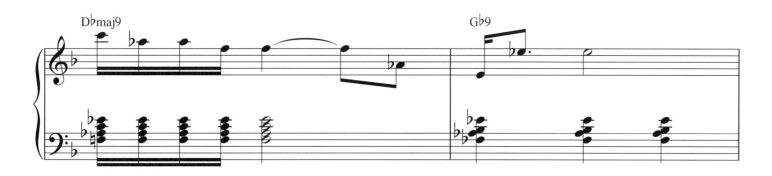

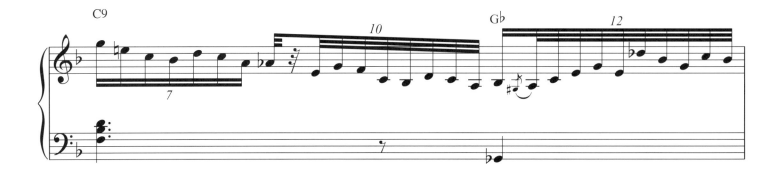

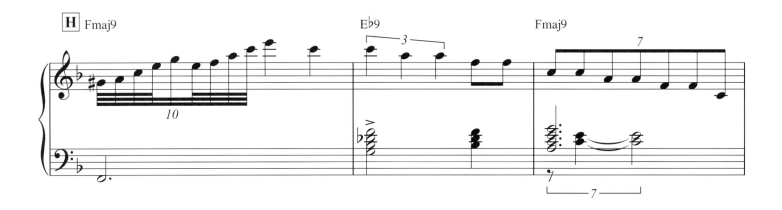

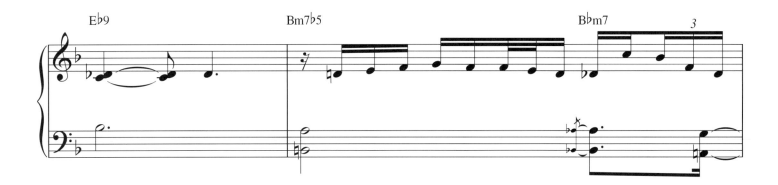

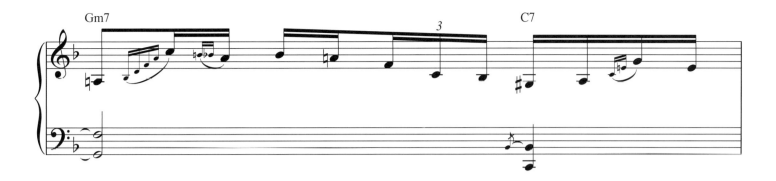

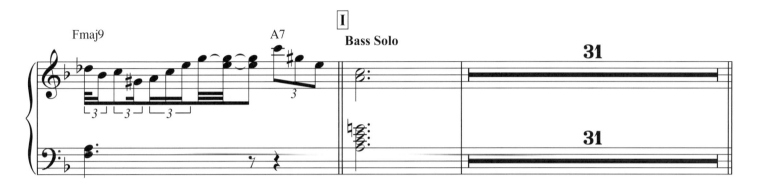

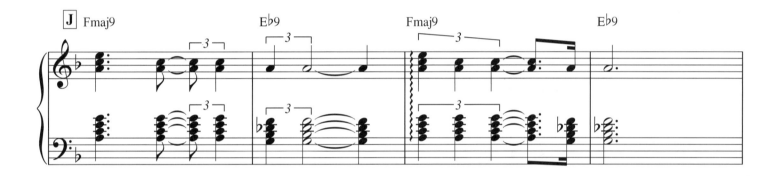

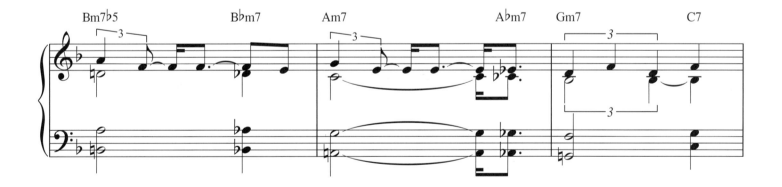

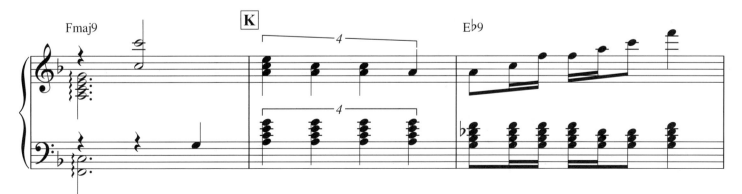

Laid Back

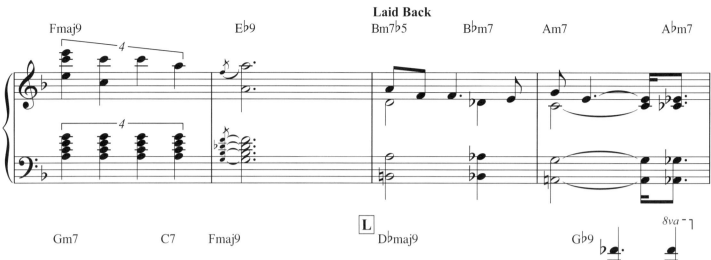

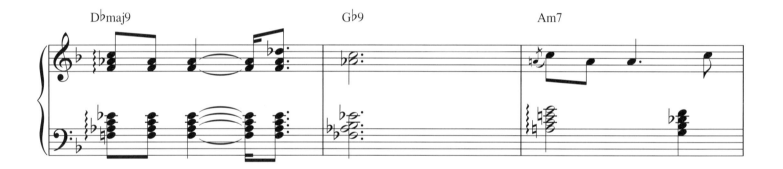

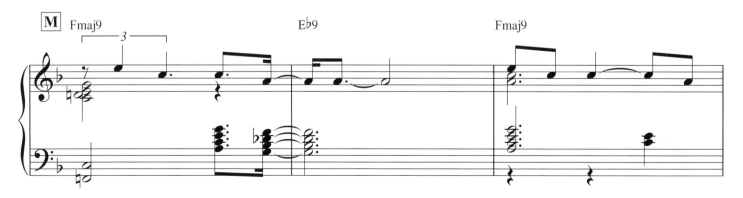

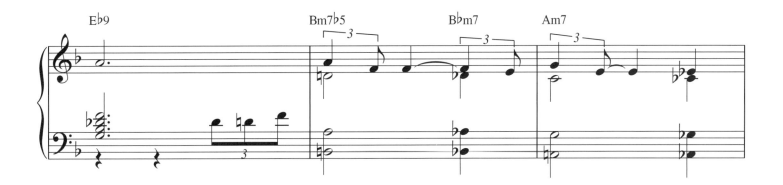

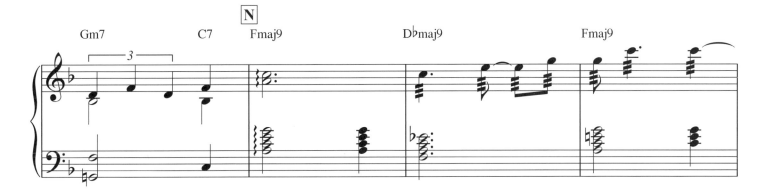

Fade Out

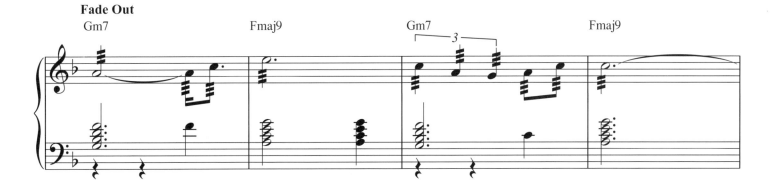

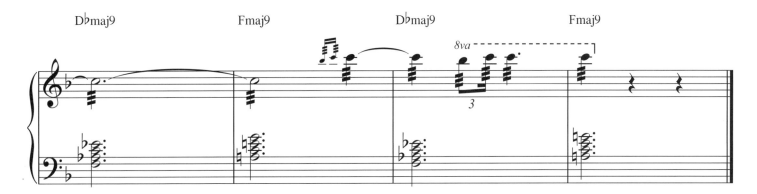

Linus and Lucy

By Vince Guaraldi

Moderately

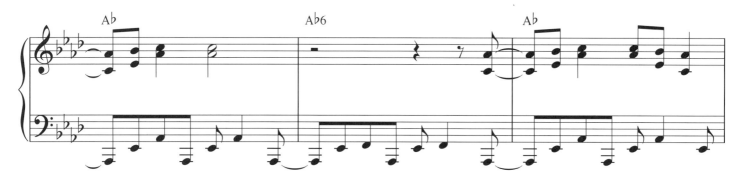

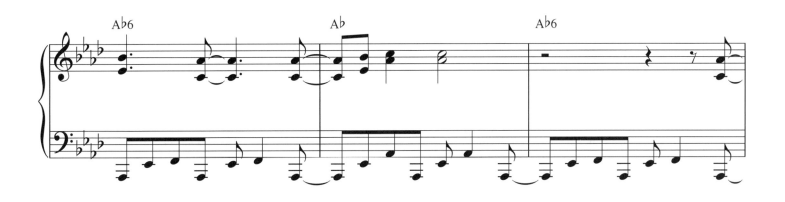

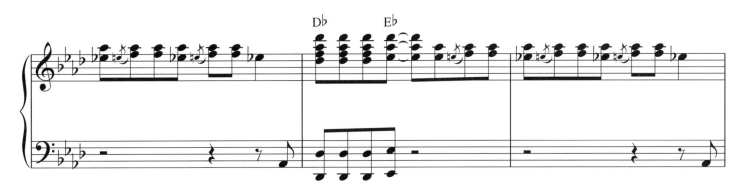

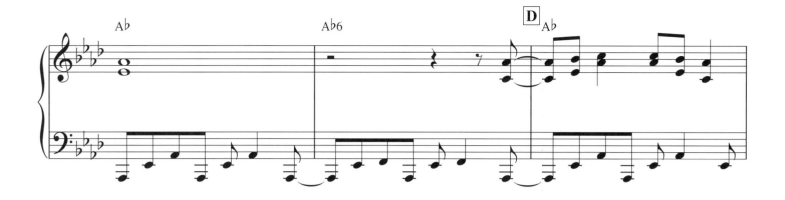

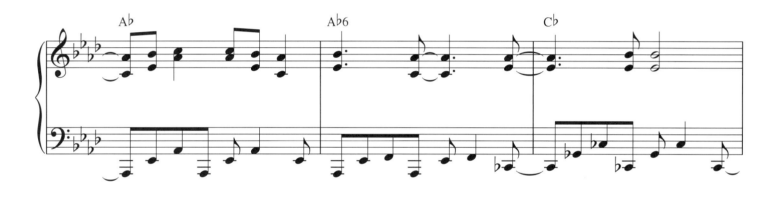

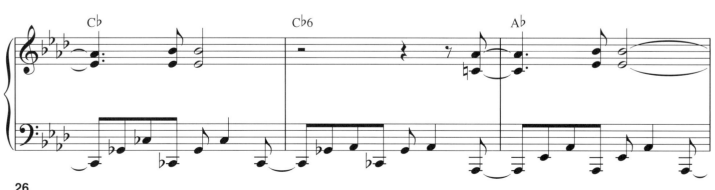

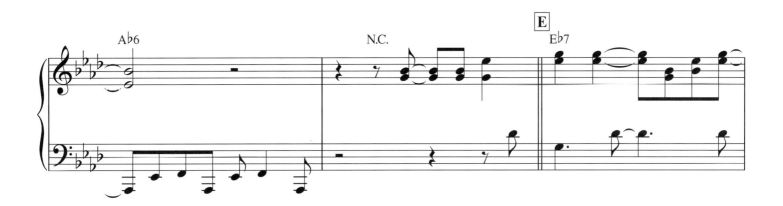

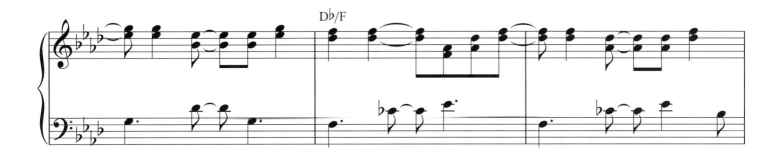

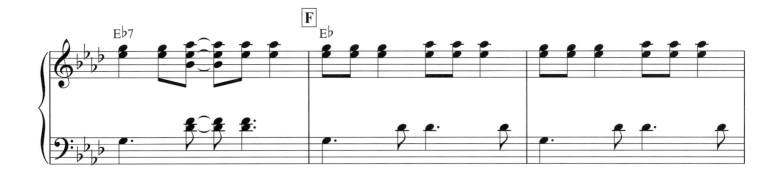

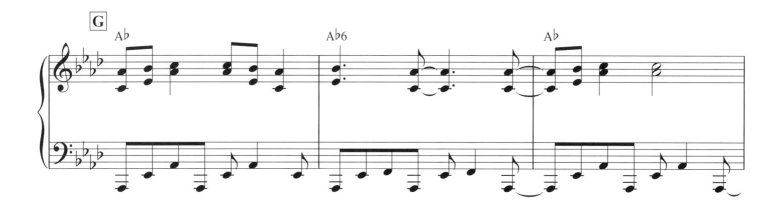

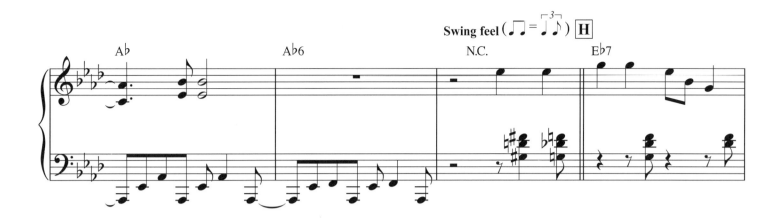

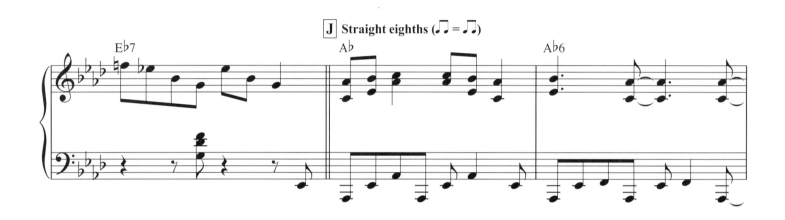

J Straight eighths (♪♪ = ♪♪)

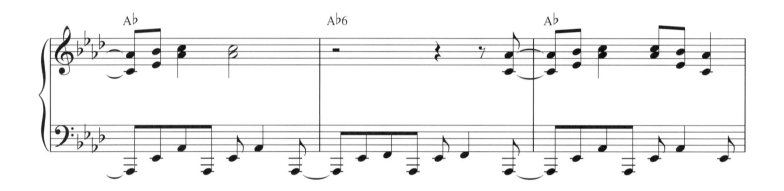

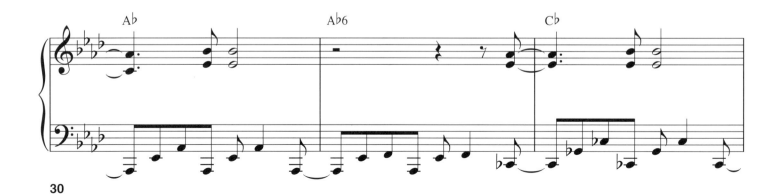

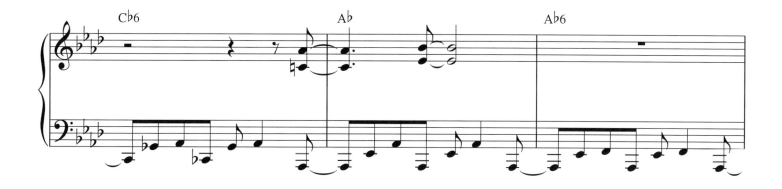

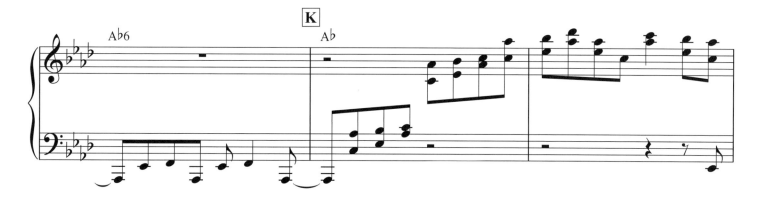

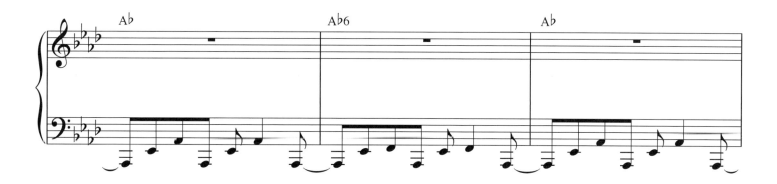

K

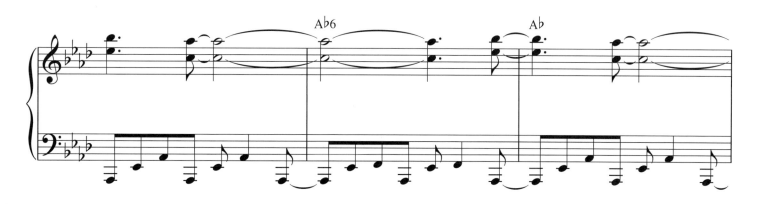

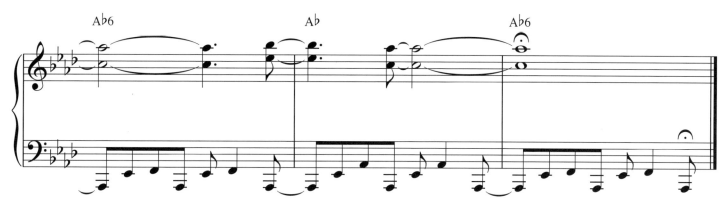

My Little Drum

By Vince Guaraldi

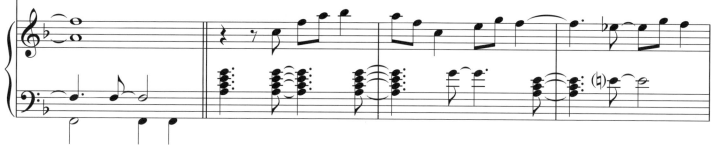

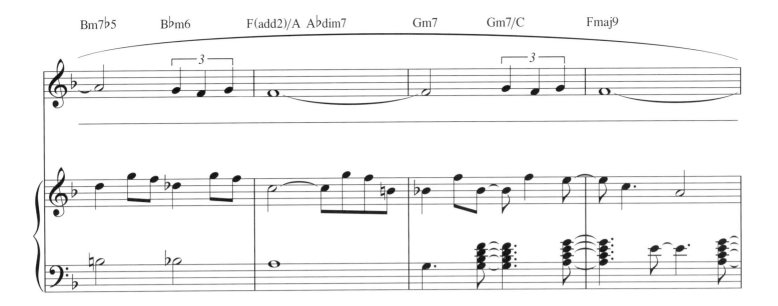

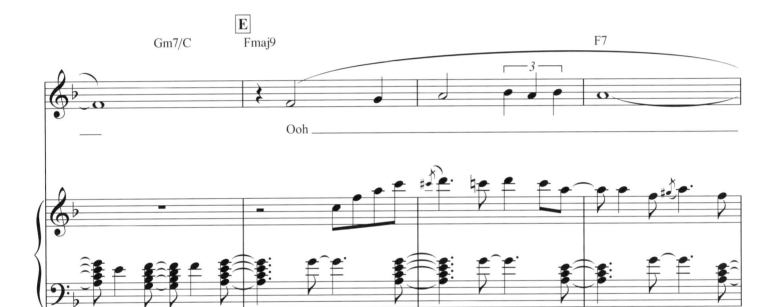

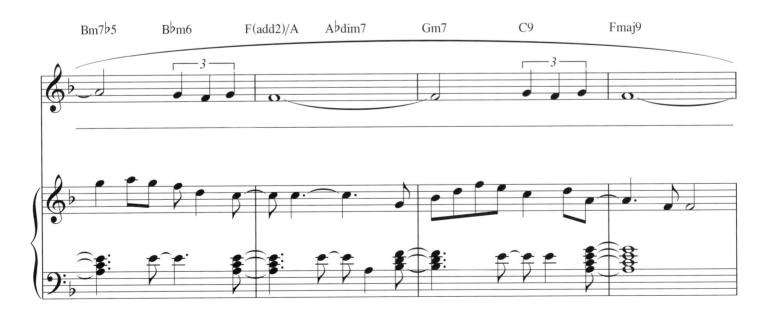

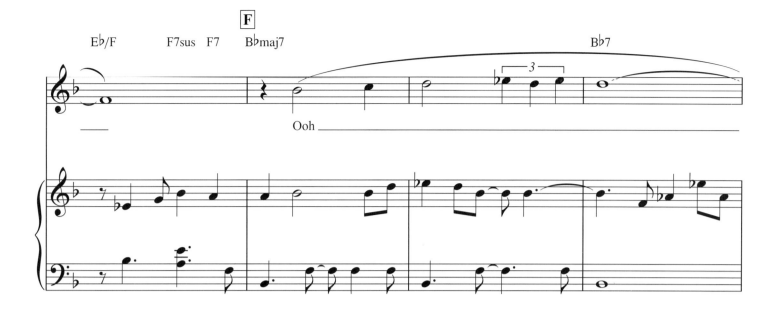

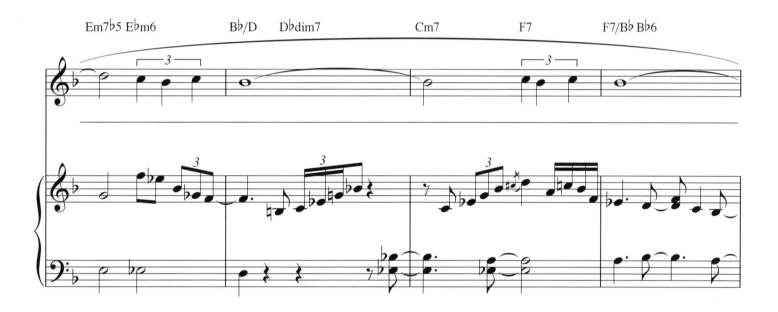

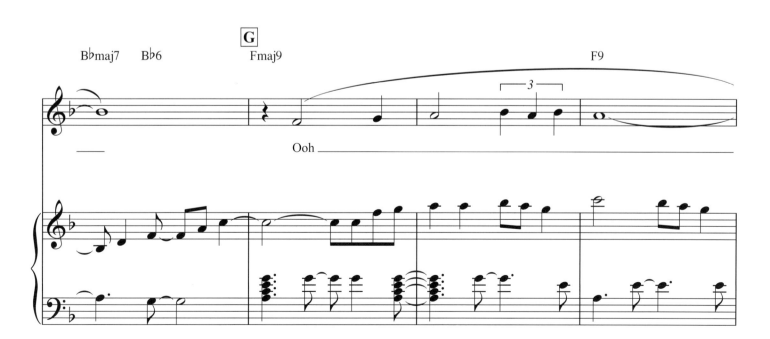

Bm7♭5   B♭m6   F/A A♭m7   Gm7 B♭m/C   Fmaj9

D.S. al Coda

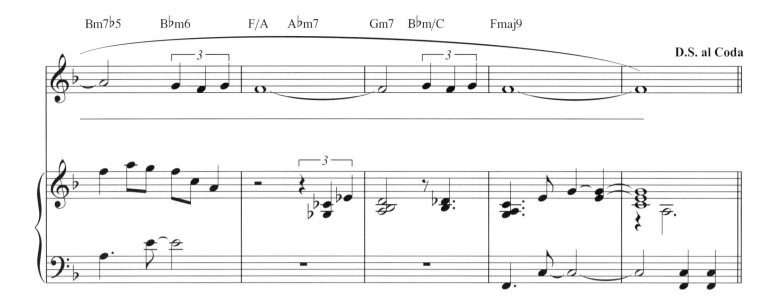

CODA   N.C./F   H

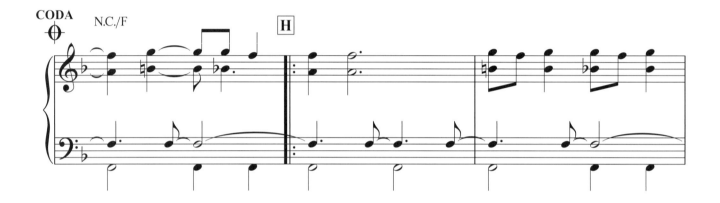

Repeat and Fade | **Optional Ending**

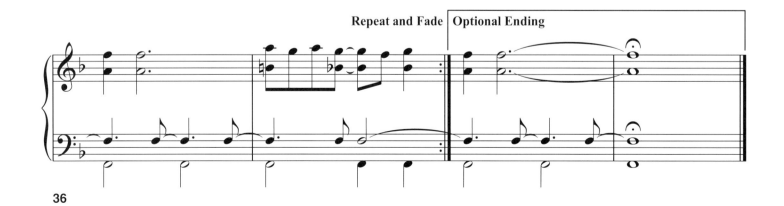

Skating

By Vince Guaraldi

Bright Jazz Waltz

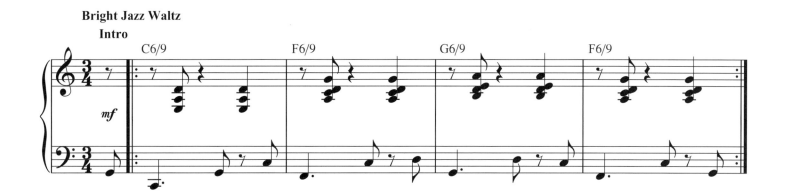

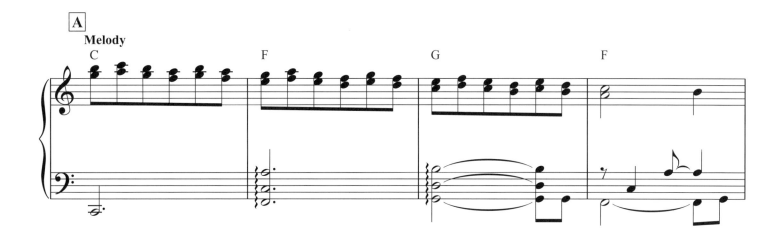

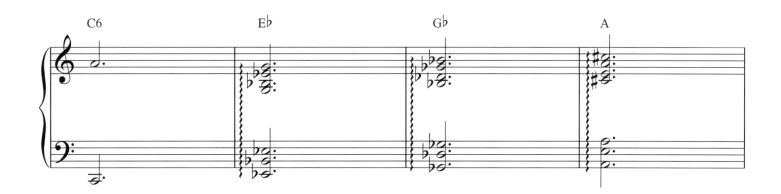

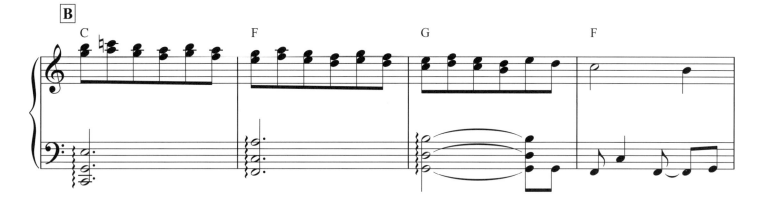

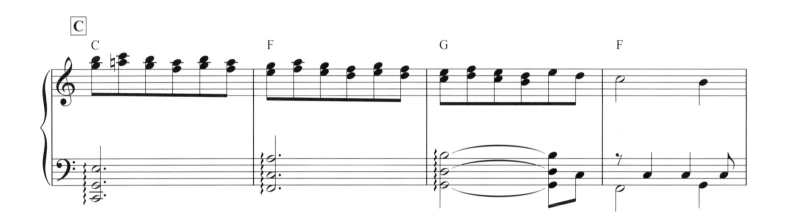

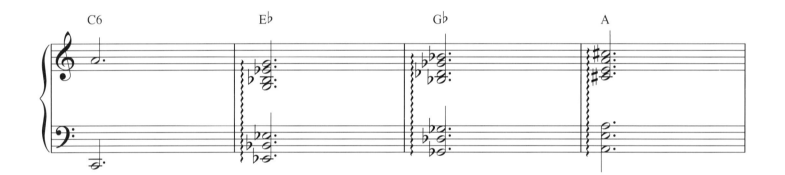

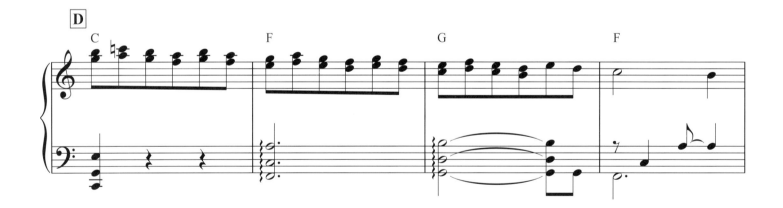

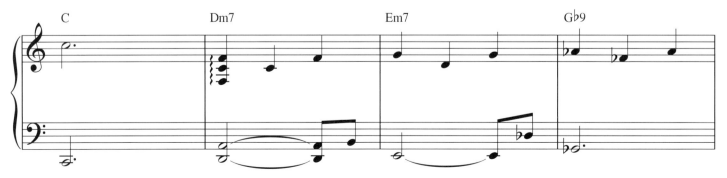

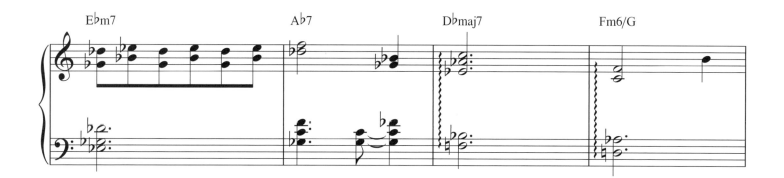

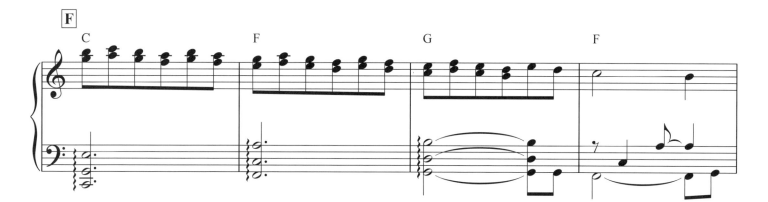

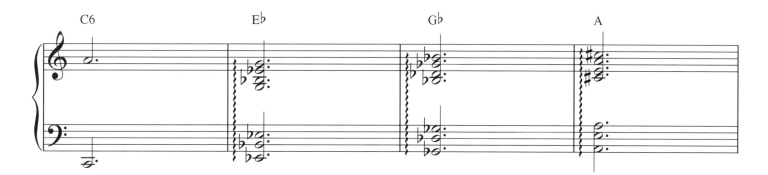

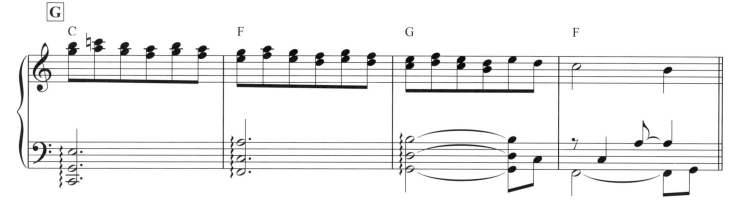

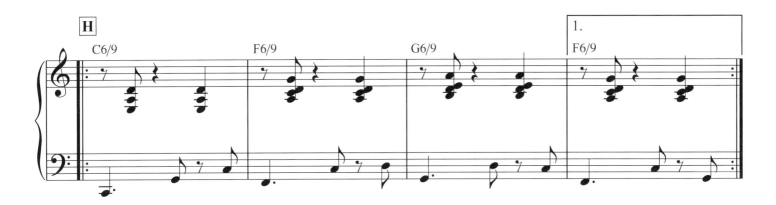

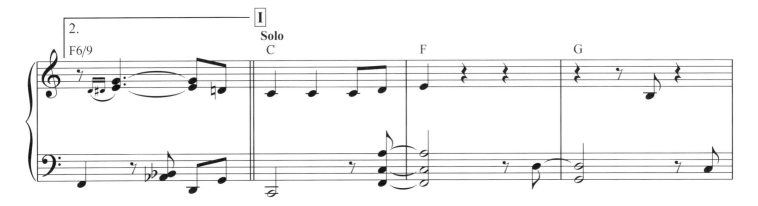

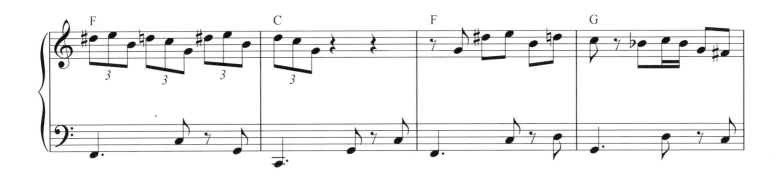

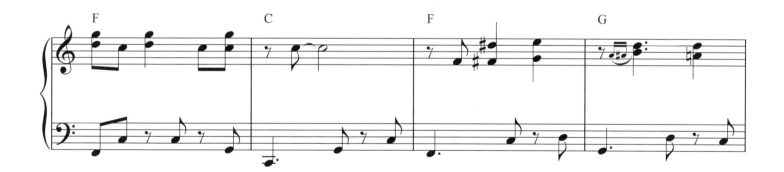

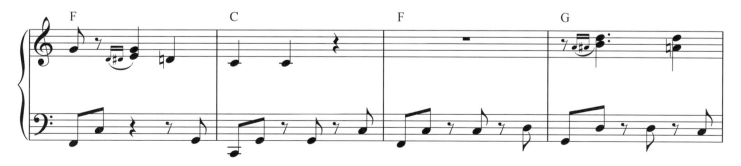

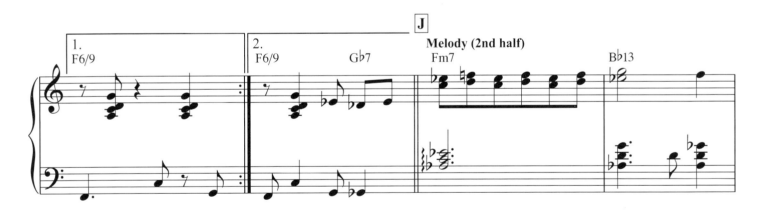

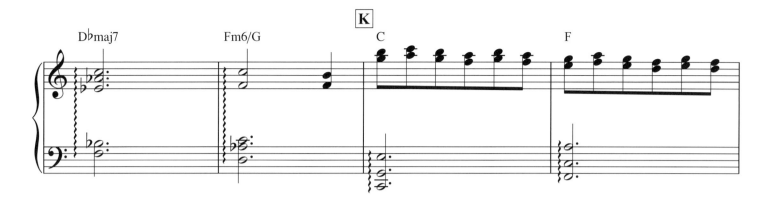

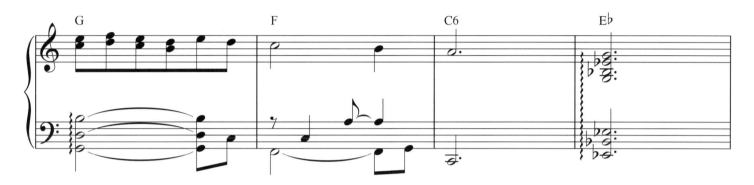

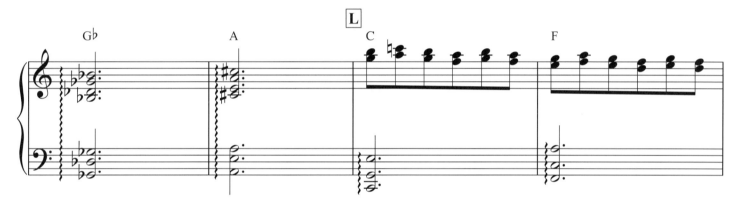

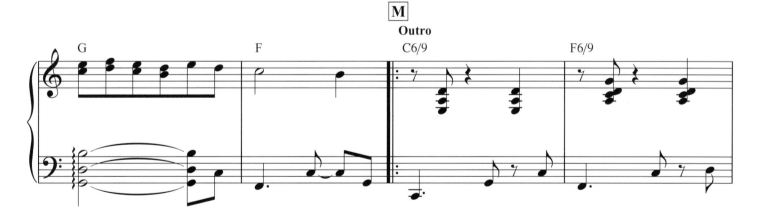

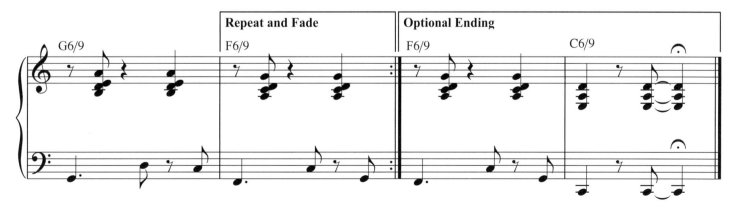

O Tannenbaum

Traditional
Arranged by Vince Guaraldi

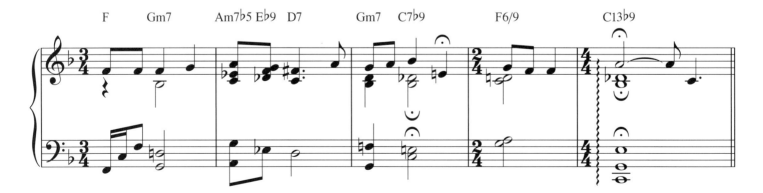

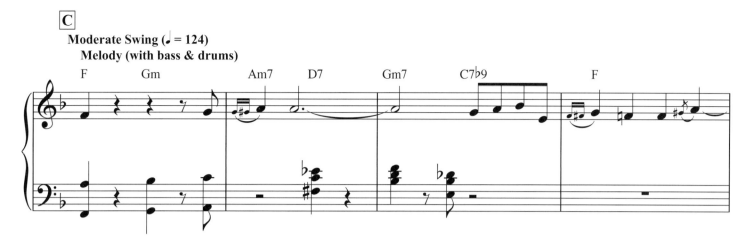

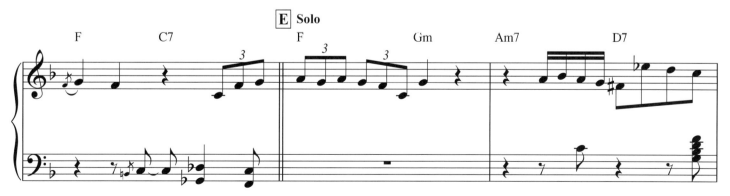

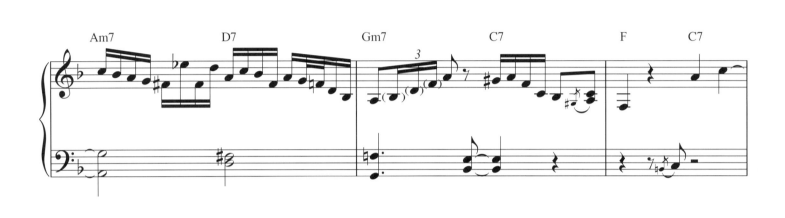

46

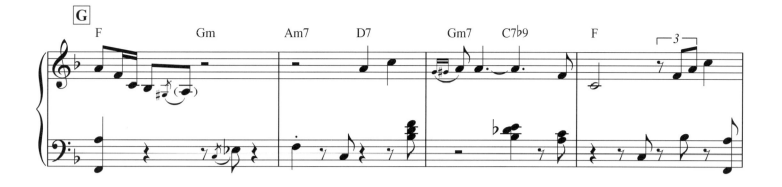

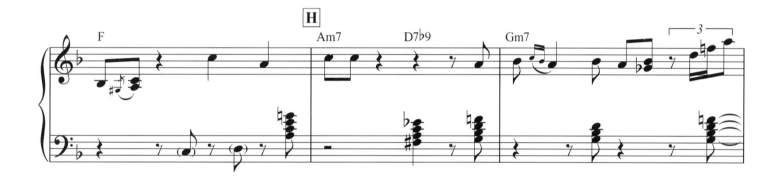

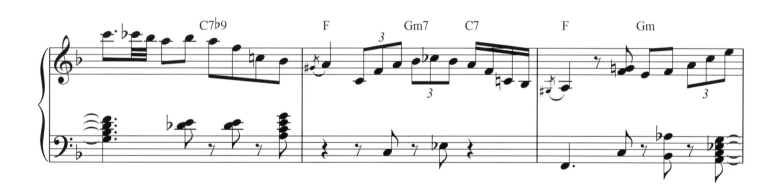

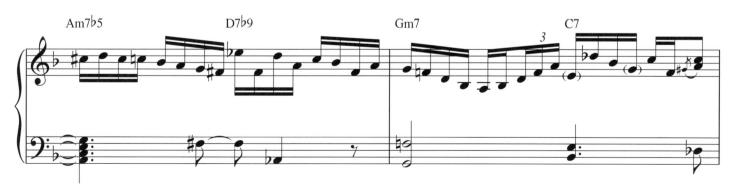

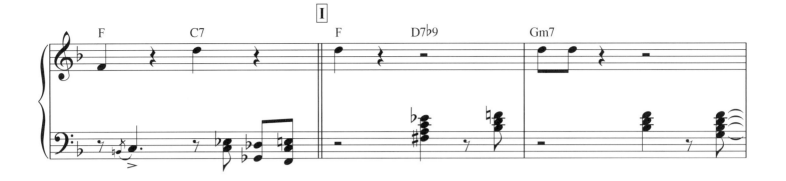

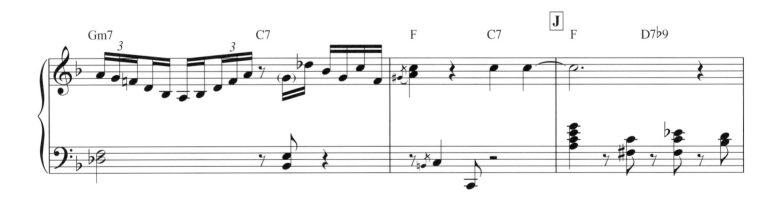

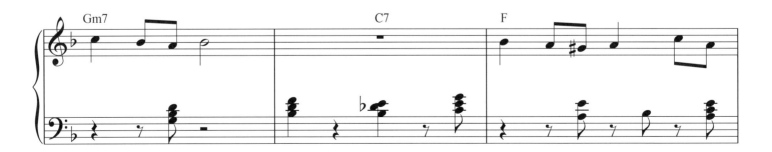

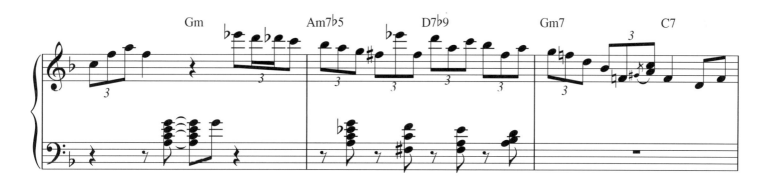

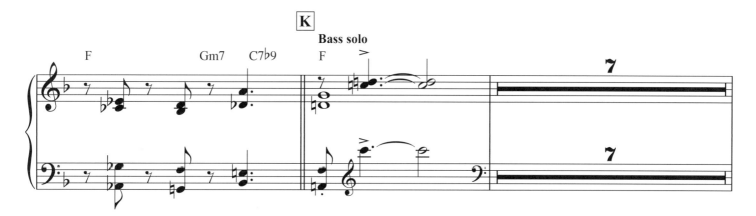

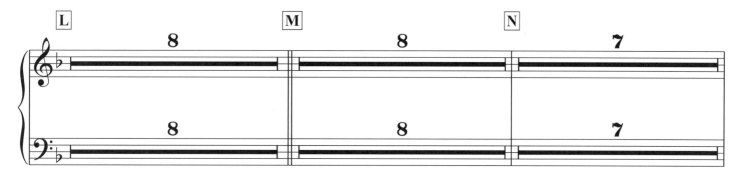

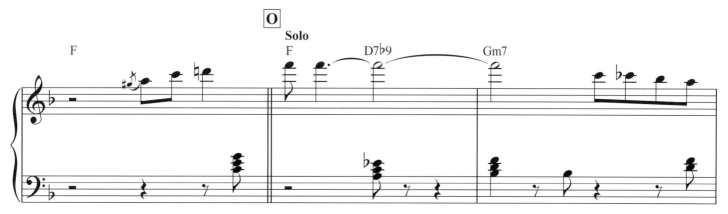

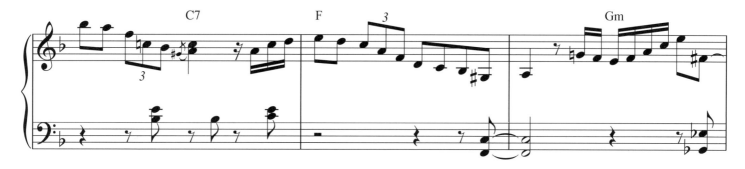

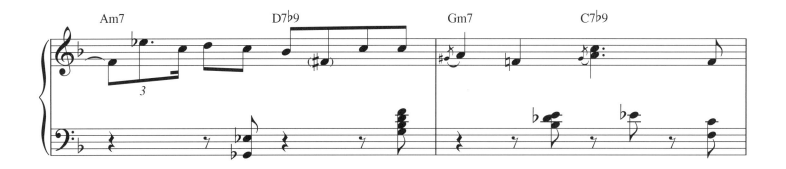

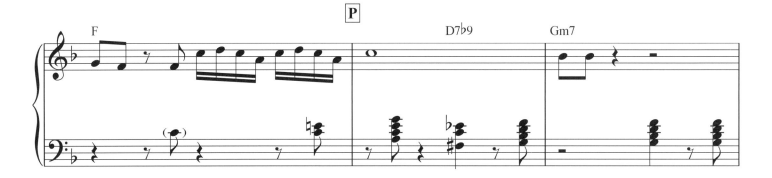

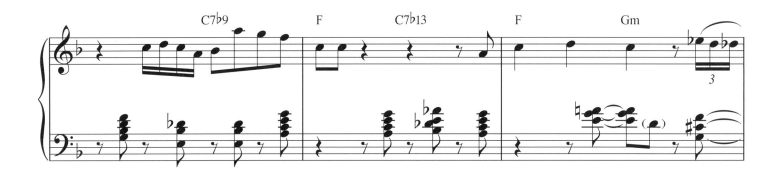

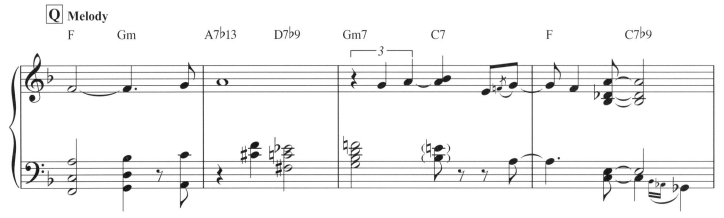

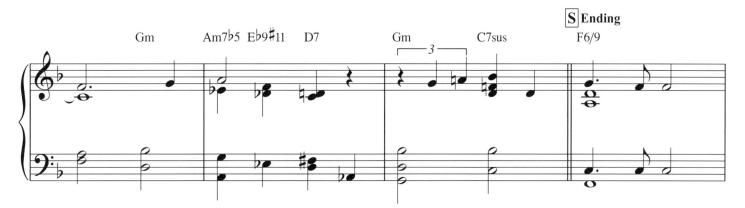

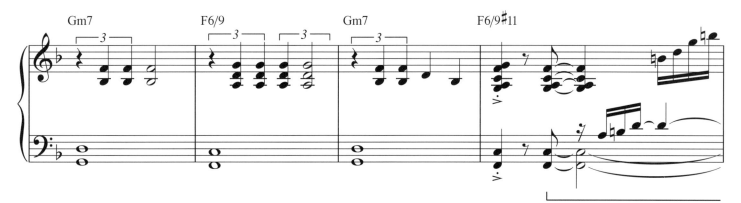

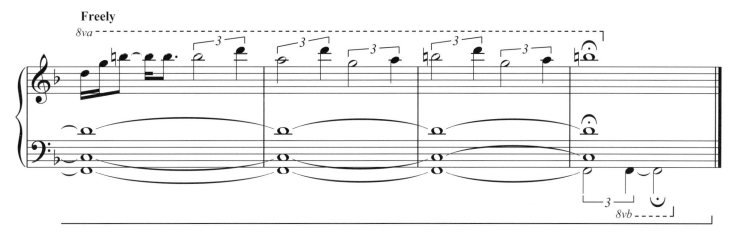

What Child Is This

Traditional
Arranged by Vince Guaraldi

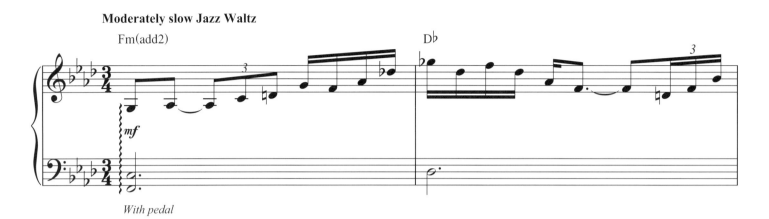

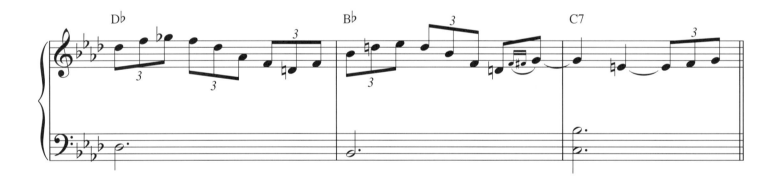

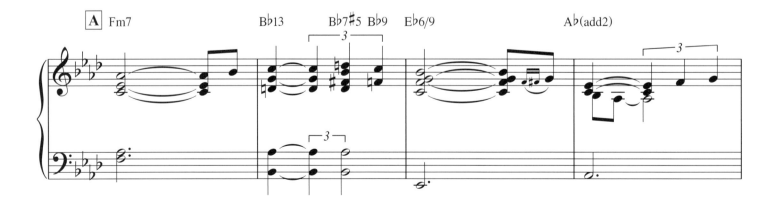

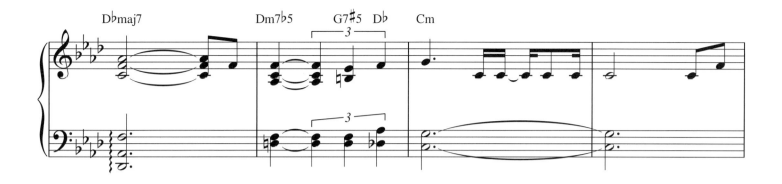

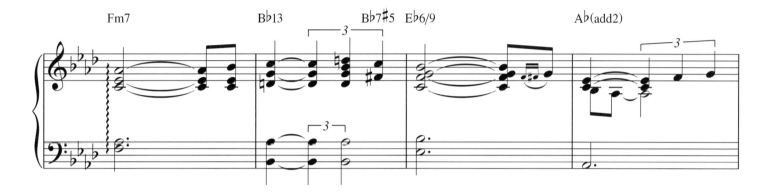

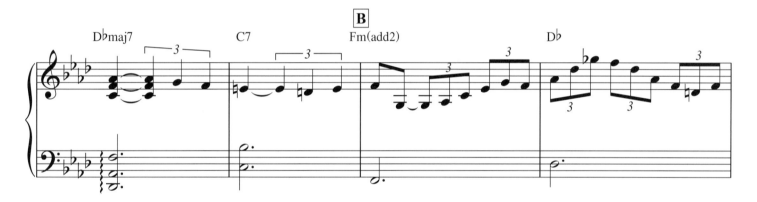

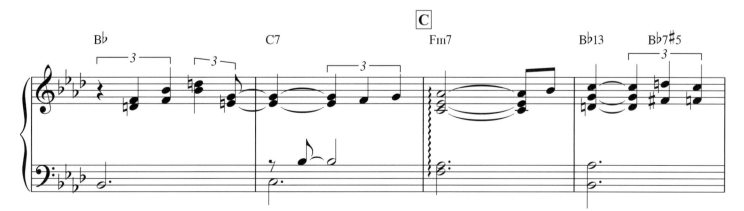

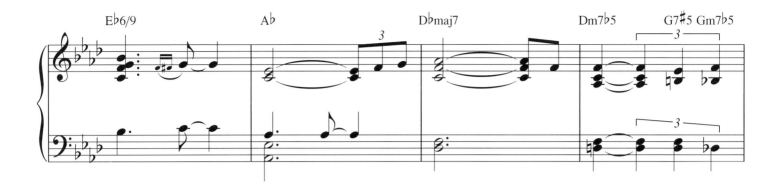

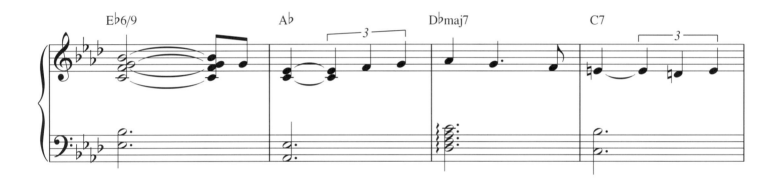

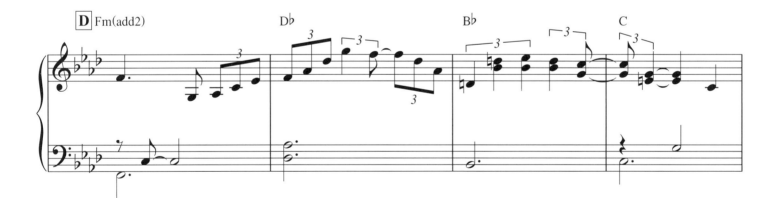

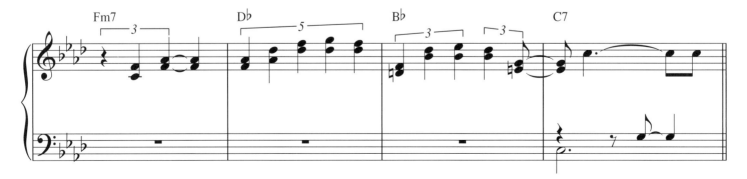

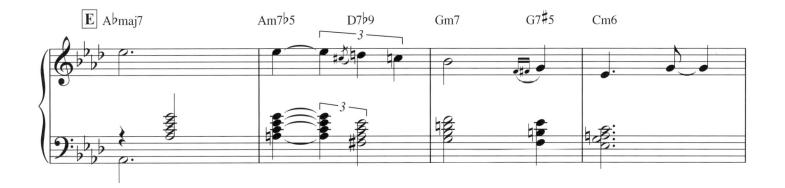

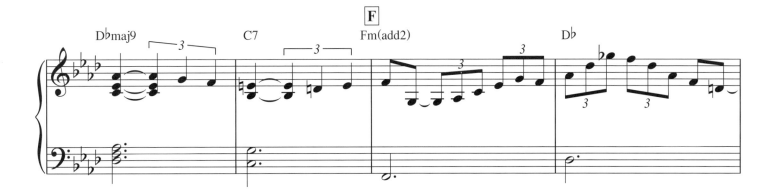

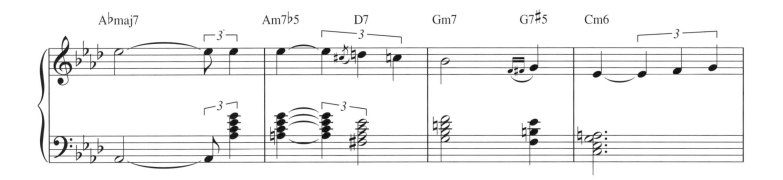

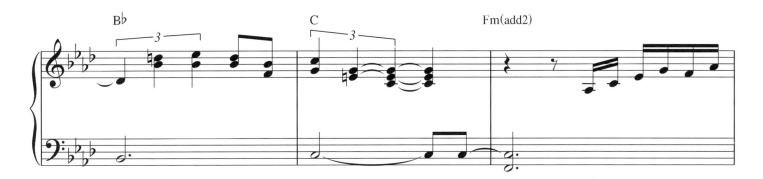

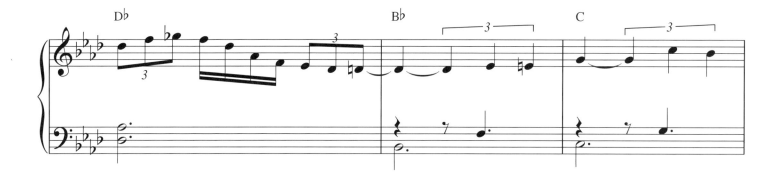

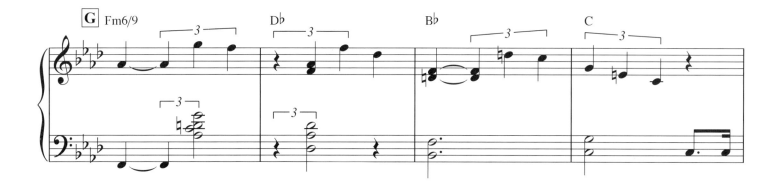

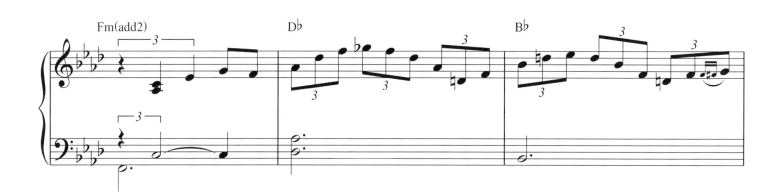

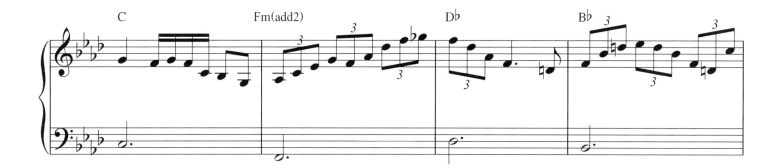

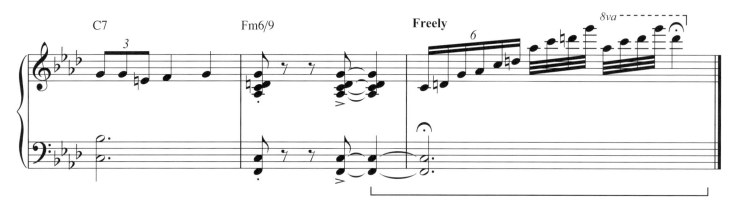